BRITAIN IN OLD PHOTOGRAPHS

CHELTENHAM IN THE 1950s

PETER GILL

SUTTON PUBLISHING LIMITED

Sutton Publishing Limited
Phoenix Mill · Thrupp · Stroud
Gloucestershire · GL5 2BU

First published 1996

British Library Cataloguing in Publication Data
A catalogue record for this book is available from the
British Library.

ISBN 0-7509-1266-9

Typeset in 10/12 Perpetua.
Typesetting and origination by
Sutton Publishing Limited.
Printed in Great Britain by
Ebenezer Baylis, Worcester

This book is dedicated to two very special young ladies, Natalie and Jessica, who get more beautiful every day – I will love them always.

A children's fancy dress party at St Barnabas' church hall in Orchard Way to celebrate the coronation of Queen Elizabeth II in 1953. The boy wearing the clown's costume (front row, left) is Tim Kent. His parents Vic (wearing glasses) and Audrey are standing behind him.

CONTENTS

Best Wishes,

The masters of Dean Close School during the Michaelmas term, 1953. Back row, left to right: D.F. Lepine (Music), G.V. Harries (History), Revd P.R.W. Tidmarsh (Chaplain), D.J. Carwill (History, Economics), A.S.R. Parker (English), D.A. Barker (Physics), H.C. Neill (Classics), E.S. Hay (Chemistry), P.J. Ridler (Modern Languages). Front row: E. Rowe (Bursar), C.J. Kennedy (Art), E.S. Hoare (Maths, Geography), Miss A. Schneider (German), F. Horsley (Maths), A.N. Gilkes (Headmaster), C.A.P. Tuckwell (English, Latin, French), F.R.H. Brian (Maths), J.S. Moore (Biology), E.H. Taylor (Science, Crafts), M.A. Girling (Geography, English, Latin).

INTRODUCTION

'The final decision in every case, good or evil, in great or small matters, always has rested, and always will, on the individual.' (Queen Elizabeth, the Queen Mother, in July 1954 during the centenary celebrations of the opening of Cheltenham Ladies' College.)

During the fifties there was much development, expansion and change in Cheltenham. It was a decade that saw much modernization of the town centre, often at the expense of classical architecture, and a time when the town started to encroach on the surrounding farmland to create sprawling conurbations.

The war had seen the emergence of a strong industrial base in the area, especially with the development of Dowty's and the relocation of Smith's Industries to Bishops Cleeve. During the fifties this base consolidated to create a healthy demand for labour. In addition the relocation of GCHQ from Bletchley Park to Cheltenham in the early part of the decade required a strong civil servant workforce, and the movement of the Eagle Star and Royal Insurance companies to the town encouraged a clerical workforce. This combination resulted in a large labour market and a veritable flood of workers moved to the town. The council embarked on an extensive housing programme to ensure adequate accommodation for its rapidly enlarging population. Consequently we see the development of estates such as Hesters Way, Benhall, Rowanfield and Lynworth, among others.

Simultaneously, the Council embarked on various projects within the town centre to modernize its image. Many Regency buildings were demolished, along with other dilapidated buildings of various periods, to make way for utilitarian blocks that were and are purely functional. It was no longer acceptable for Cheltenham to be a Regency Spa town, lost in its past heritage. Now the town had to embrace the twentieth century and provide all that a modern town should.

Many of the developments that were built at this time are today, forty years on, deemed dated, characterless and tasteless. Already we want to change the shape and image of Princess Elizabeth Way and Hester's Way, the Royal Well bus terminus is constantly threatened with demolition, and all around the town it seems that the buildings of the fifties are in a worse state of repair and decoration than the finer, and much older buildings.

The fifties saw Cheltenham's status change from a 'country town' to a 'modern town in the Cotswolds'. This was almost solely due to the war and the subsequent development of some of the best engineering firms in the country. The developments of the fifties made Cheltenham the town it is today. Even though we are now trying to restore the character and flavour of the town's Regency zenith, and lose the image that was created in the fifties and sixties, it is largely because of these attempts at modernization that we have a modern and popular town today. Throughout the country, towns were destroyed and 'recreated' during this time in much the same way, and Cheltenham's Council followed the trend. Though we may despair of such architecture today and weep for the buildings we lost (such as the Boys' Grammar School in the Lower High Street), we must still acknowledge that this modernization was in many ways important for the development of the town. It was necessary for Cheltenham to 'feel' modern for it to become modern, and therefore to develop. Only now that Cheltenham has an acknowledged status as a tourist town, a home for music and literature festivals, a focus for the racing fraternity, and as a centre of shopping excellence, can it relax, be confident of its identity and start once more to create the fine exteriors of classic architecture. Cheltenham no longer needs the false trappings of 'modern' characterless architecture so essential in the fifties because it is, and it knows that it is, a modern, characterful and classic British town, but it had to go through that process in order to develop in the way that it has.

This book is much more than just a look at the buildings and architecture of Cheltenham during the fifties, although the development and growth of this aspect plays an important role. It is also, where relevant photographs have been available, a look at the town through its schools, sport, drama, children and special events. In compiling a book like this it seems there are all too few facts to go with the photographs, but I have attempted to put together an honest look at life in Cheltenham during a decade of change.

Inevitably, I have missed some important facts; there are names I cannot put to faces, and information is missing from the captions owing to my lack of knowledge in certain areas. If people can add to or correct what I have written, I would be most grateful to hear from them and learn more of this subject: please write to me and help keep the history of our town alive.

As a last note, I would like to thank the unknown lady who gave me, via my father, the photograph and information on Vladimir Lavinski. Unfortunately my father has forgotten her name. I would very much like to hear from her if possible.

My sincere wish is that you enjoy this book: maybe it will bring back memories; maybe it will give a deeper insight into the town that so many people visit or live in today.

Peter Gill, July 1996

A 1920 Belsize 014027 on a VCC test run on the Cheltenham road coming into Bishops Cleeve, 9 July 1955. Behind is a car of similar vintage on the same test run. The Newland Inn whose sign is visible on the right was bought by Smith's Industries in the early 1960s and duly pulled down so that the factory could continue to expand. The main road junction on the Cheltenham Road by Smith's is still generally referred to as the 'Newland's Crossroads'. During the 1950s Mr Hancock owned the small cottage on the left.

CHILDREN OF THE 1950s

Proud mothers with the winning babies of the bonny baby competition outside the Pump Rooms in 1956. These were the birth–9 months age group. The first prize winner was Pamela Harrison (third from left) who is being held by her mother.

The junior class of Charlton Kings Primary School, *c.* 1959. The children were photographed in their last summer term at the school before they headed off to their secondary education.

Girls of the Ladies' College collecting their school sacks as they prepare for the day's lessons. The sacks were made by the firm of S. Rouse and Co. of Gloucester Road and are as much a part of the students' equipment today as they were in the 1950s. Indeed S. Rouse and Co. still make the sacks to the same specifications. The girls' names were stencilled on to the front along with their house. The uniform has also changed very little: Lovat green coats and skirts, brown stockings and pale green felt hats, the last-named being no longer worn. This uniform was first introduced by Margaret E. Popham when she was appointed principal in 1937; previously the girls were attired in navy tunics, black stockings and black velour hats with wide hatbands. Miss Popham was a charismatic and forceful headmistress, who finally retired from the college in 1953; she was replaced by Miss J.A. Tredgold.

The Revd Douglas L. Graham, headmaster of Dean Close School, with an older pupil, March 1956. Graham served the school as headmaster from 1954 until 1968. He had already enjoyed a varied career – after seven years as a master at Eton College between the wars this popular Southern Irishman resigned in order to become a Chaplain in the Royal Navy for the last four years of the Second World War.

One of the fieldcrafts taught during the 1950s at Dean Close School was stone-walling. Here Roger Grimshaw is being tutored by F.R.H. Brian, a master more usually found in the mathematics classroom or out bird-watching.

These young artists at Dean Close School are being tutored by Cedric Kennedy, a very talented and locally famous water-colourist. On the left is Guy Palmer, on the right Anthony Miller.

These boys of Dean Close School were members of the young farmers club at the school in 1956 and were required to look after the pigs kept in a sty on school grounds. Left to right: P.M. Maxwell Jones, J.P. Sedgwick, R.D. Harding.

Actors rehearsing 'Much Ado About Nothing' in 1952 in the outdoor theatre at Dean Close School, now named the Tuckwell Theatre after its founder, C.A.P. Tuckwell. Seated on the left, directing the actors, is C.A.P. Tuckwell himself, who took the part of Benedick. The master standing on the left is H.N. Neill as Leonardo, T.R. Morgan, dressed in white, is Claudio, and standing at the back on the right is A.T. Goodchild.

A service in progress in the chapel at Dean Close School in March 1956. The red-brick chapel was designed by architect L.W. Barnard and was officially opened on 1 November 1923. The chaplain in 1956 was the Revd P.R.W. Tidmarsh. The organist (left) is David Lepine who was director of music at Dean Close from 1953 to 1961; he later went on to be organist/music director at the new Coventry Cathedral. The organ that Mr Lepine is playing was bought second-hand in 1951 from St Mary's Church, Charlton Kings, and is a 2-manual pipe organ.

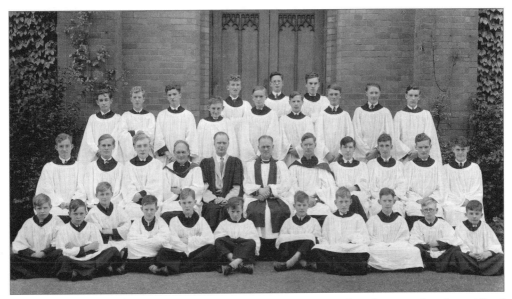

The Dean Close school choir, 1953. The chaplain, the Revd P.R.W. Tidmarsh, is seated in the middle of the second row. He succeeded the Revd E.V. Tanner in 1951 and remained at the school until 1958 when the Revd R. Walters took over for a brief period. To the left of Mr Tidmarsh is the English teacher, Arnold Parker, and on his other side is Derek Gaze, the director of music.

The Dean Close School CCF Officers and NCOs, 1952. Back row, left to right: J.G. Mayes, M.L. Spragg, A.L. MacNair, C. Hicks, D.S. Marriott, D.S. Peacock, R.F. Knight, M. Smith, J.M. George, C.T. Jones, M.R. Greening. Middle row: C.D. Cecil, D.B. Roberts, D.J. Burrage, M.J. Stock, J. Porter-Wright, D.W. Jones, D.V. Rose, H.T. Clements, J.H. Lutley, M.G. Dash, R.C.M. Melville, R.T.C. Rowley, B.A.E. Chapman. Front row: A.T. Goodchild, G.D. Inkin, C.L. Hodgetts, E.S. Hay, D. Gaye, A.S.R. Parker, A.W. Golder MBE, C.B. Kiddell, P.R.W. Tidmarsh, W.T.M. Murphy, T.R. Morgan, N.J.H. Dodds. In 1952 there were 230 cadets, divided into army and RAF sections.

A junior prefect of the Gentlemen's College Junior School welcoming Princess Elizabeth to the junior school during her visit to the town and college on Friday 15 March 1951. The college headmaster, A.G. Elliot-Smith, stands by the car, while the junior school headmaster, Mr H. Clutton-Brock, stands with his wife behind the boys.

In one of the woodwork shops of the college a pupil presents the Princess with a handmade gift for her young son Prince Charles.

The Princess was escorted around the main college by a group of prefects, as young college photographers played the part of the paparazzi. The prefects are, from left to right: J.R.L. Harman, C.D. Evans, A.B. Carles, J.C. Boutflower, G.E.L. Williams, P.N. Trim, A. Whitehorn.

Junior school boys applauding as the Princess leaves after her visit to the school. The two headmasters follow behind.

Members of the St John's Ambulance before going off to summer camp, early in the 1950s. The children were given lessons in first aid and home nursing, and were encouraged to take examinations and badges. At this time the St John's headquarters was in the Gloucester Road.

Children of the Bennington Street Non-Denominational Sunday School pose for the camera after performing their Christmas show, c. 1955.

The cast from a 'Sunbeam' pantomime in the 1950s. The Sunbeams were a young theatrical group organized and run by Mrs Winnie Townsend to raise money for charity. They staged regular shows for which Mrs Townsend made the costumes, accompanied the singing on the piano, and choreographed the dancing. Rehearsals for the shows were held at Whaddon School or upstairs in the Crown and Cushion, Bath Road. Performances were held in Prestbury and St Michael's Church Hall, Severn Road. Betty Smith (née Gill) is on the right of the front row.

Another Sunbeam production. Mrs Townsend, who lived for many years at 21 Hillview, St Mark's, first started her productions while working in Stroud as a teacher during the First World War. She invited wounded soldiers who were billeted nearby to come to her school productions; they enjoyed it so much that she decided to do further concert parties. After the war she stopped the concerts for a while, but during the Second World War, when she was living in Cheltenham and working as a dinner lady at Leckhampton Primary School, she began the concerts again with a production in Prestbury.

The Sunbeams continued their productions throughout the 1950s and into the 1960s until Winnie Townsend was unable to organize any more. Sixth from the left is Barbara Gill (née Williams), and the girl singing on her right is Betty Smith (née Gill).

The girl wearing the tiara (front row, centre) is Sandra Mason (née Gill), following in the footsteps of her older sister Betty who was also a Sunbeam. Winnie Townsend's one main rule and regulation was that only young girls were allowed in her productions. She refused to let boys take part.

Another Sunbeam pantomime. The company also gave many concerts and concert parties. They performed wherever they were asked or invited, from community centres to hospitals and old people's homes.

Three prominent Sunbeams of the 1950s, photographed in 1954. The little girl is Sandra Mason (née Gill), on the left is Betty Smith (née Gill) and on the right is Barbara Gill (née Williams), who married Michael Gill, the sisters' older brother.

CHELTENHAM'S BUSINESSES

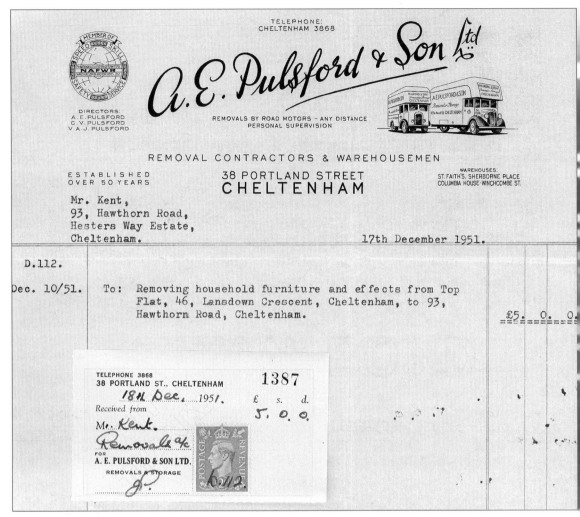

Pulsford's offices were at 38 Portland Street; by the 1950s this was a well-established firm with over fifty years' experience. Throughout the war they worked for the Air Ministry and Ministry of Aircraft Production. During the '50s their removal vans were painted cream with blue writing.

Elliott Bros was another removal firm working in Cheltenham at this time. This company was formed by the brothers F.R. and A.J. Elliott just after the First World War as haulage merchants and coal hauliers. Their first vehicles were horse-drawn, and continued to be used until 1964.

In the 1950s, Elliott Bros also operated as transport contractors, with their headquarters in Prince's Street, Cheltenham. In 1949 Elliott Brothers became a limited company with the sons and daughters of the founders becoming its directors. The Chevrolet truck painted here was bought new by the firm in 1959 from Haines & Strange, who supplied Elliotts with new Chevrolets from 1931.

A minor accident involving an Elliott Bros lorry; the driver misjudged the angle on to the bridge and collided with the bridge wall.

Employees of Elliott Bros pose in the Bouncer's Lane yard with the new fleet truck in 1959. Left to right: Frank Paget, Charlie Critchley, Eric Johnson, Dennis Birdsall.

Mrs Brian Elliott with an open-backed truck bought by the company on 31 May 1957. Her husband now runs B. Elliott & Sons from Bishops Cleeve.

Between 1951 and 1953 the Black and White Bus Company modernized their fleet by purchasing thirty-one of these Leyland Royal Tigers. These coaches were fitted with thirty-three seats in a 'Willowbrook' body, and they were noted for their reliable engines although their braking was always unpredictable. The company operated these coaches throughout the 1950s and into the mid-1960s, serving the Express Network service linking Cheltenham to most parts of the country. This vehicle, No. 142, is preparing to set off for Weymouth. (*Courtesy C.F. Martin Collection*)

The Cheltenham-based firm of Kearseys ran several factory bus services throughout the 1950s, notably to the Gloster Aircraft Company at Brockworth and Rotol at Staverton. They also ran some county services to Winchcombe, Bishops Cleeve, Guiting and Stow. Several Daimler buses like the one pictured here were acquired from Birmingham Corporation and served throughout the decade. Bus No. 67 is shown at the Prestbury Road bus depot. (*Courtesy C.F. Martin Collection*)

A 1948 Bristol K bus (left) and a Stratford Blue Leyland PD1, belonging to the Bristol Tramways Bus Company fleet at the Royal Well bus station before its rebuild. With the nationalization of road passenger transport throughout the country in 1950, the Cheltenham-based Red and White Company, along with Western National, handed over their mid-Gloucestershire operations to the Bristol Tramways and Carriage Company. Initially the local buses looked the same, with the red and cream livery being retained; the most noticeable change in the short term was the fitting of rear indicators to all the buses. Later Bristol Tramways became Bristol Omnibus, the northern area of which became the Cheltenham & Gloucester Omnibus Company in 1983. In 1994 this company was in turn taken over by Stagecoach. (*Courtesy C.F. Martin Collection*)

Mr R.A. Gill attaching his Driving Instructor plates to his Mini outside his home at Oakbank, Hayes Road, Cheltenham. Mr Gill ran the Lansdown School of Motoring from Salem House in Clarence Parade during the 1950s and taught many people to drive in this very Mini.

The fleet of Gloucestershire Dairy milk-carts at the company's Prestbury Road site in the late 1950s. In the background can be seen the floodlights of the Cheltenham Town football ground and slightly in front of them are the roofs of prefabs.

Every day some 60,000 pints of milk would pass through the Gloucestershire Dairy in Imperial Lane in the late 1950s. The dairy was opened in 1876 as a small cake shop in the Promenade by Mrs Holborrow. By the end of the 1950s the business still owned the original shop as well as two farms, the dairy shown here, the Prestbury Road site shown above, nine shops in Cheltenham and Cirencester, and additional dairies in Cirencester and Painswick.

One of the Gloucestershire Dairy's farms was Northfield Farm, which was managed by Mr David McLellan (centre). He is shown talking to Mr Austin Starforth, the managing director of the company during the 1950s. On the left is Miss Judith Manning who worked as a dairymaid at the farm. At this time Northfield Farm produced 170 gallons of milk every day.

The Gloucestershire Dairy shop on the Cirencester road in Cheltenham. The company's importance and influence was established over a long period. In 1925 it was one of the first dairies to introduce Tuberculin testing and in 1928 was one of the first in Cheltenham to introduce pasteurization. By the late 1950s the firm was introducing the mechanization that would gradually revolutionize the business and increase output by almost 20 per cent.

The entrance to Dowty Equipment Ltd on a cold winter's morning in the late 1950s. The firm had grown rapidly and successfully during the Second World War, and the 1950s were a period of great change as George Dowty intelligently began to look for diversification opportunities to ensure the survival and growth of his company.

George Dowty sought particularly to diversify into areas and industries where he felt that hydraulics could be most useful, such as in the mining industry. This coach and trailer belonged to Dowty Mining Equipment, which became an autonomous unit responsible for its own production in 1954, although both companies remained under the control of Dowty's managing director, J.A.W. Mills MBE.

George Dowty was given the Freedom of Cheltenham at a ceremony held at the Town Hall on 10 January 1954. He was the first industrialist to receive Cheltenham's highest honour, and was proclaimed an 'Honorary Freeman of the Borough of Cheltenham'. In 1956 George Dowty's outstanding services to industry were further recognized when he was awarded a knighthood in the Birthday Honours list.

During the 1940s and 1950s two of the most influential managers of Smith's Industries in Bishops Cleeve were the works director W.E. Watson MBE (left) and Ben Havilland OBE. They are shown here on Friday 13 March 1953 at a dinner held by Smith's to celebrate the award of Watson's MBE. As Smith's expanded during the 1950s they involved themselves in various local projects. In one case they gave £5,000 of financial aid towards the restoration and conversion of the Bishops Cleeve tithe barn into a village hall.

Like Dowty's, Smith's had to diversify and cast a wider net to catch their market after the war. The instruments in the interior of this 1950 Miles Gemini light twin aircraft (above), are in direct contrast to those in the far more complex Airspeed Ambassador (Elizabethan) airliner of 1955 (below). All the instruments were produced at Smiths. By the mid-1950s the Cheltenham division of Smith's Industries employed some 2,500 people, they had already established a training centre for apprentices, and a fourth factory, CH4, had been built. Most of these developments were guided by the managers, Watson and Havilland; they were greatly missed after W.E. Watson died suddenly on 14 July 1959 and Ben Havilland retired later in the same year.

In 1951 Smith's opened a technical school, which was largely run as a full-time day school with a principal, Professor Indermühle, a board of governors and full-time teaching staff. The intention was to create, on an apprenticeship basis, a well-trained and modern workforce capable of coping with the technical and scientific developments being made. Initially the school was based in the CH2 block, which housed the bench lathes with overhead countershafting belt drives shown above.

The fitting benches and precision turning benches in the technical school's new location at CH3. All Smith's factory blocks are numbered, the 'CH' prefix denoting Cheltenham. Initially the school was for fifteen to seventeen year olds, with an entrance examination held every July. No fees were payable for the course which lasted three years and combined theory and practical work.

An important part of Smith's Industries throughout the 1950s was the production of clocks and watches. This is a clock assembly room in the early 1950s; note how well the benches are illuminated. In 1953 Smith's entered a new field, producing guided weapons in the new factory block, CH4. Because of the nature of this work, the factory was given an extra security fence and in 1954 the section began to operate as a self-contained unit.

Smith's employees outside CH1 in 1957. Left to right: 'Lil', Marie Pycenic, 'Muriel', 'Paul', 'Lana', Dave Johnstone, Dennis Clark, Elsie Wesson, Sam Thomas. CH1 was the first factory built in Bishops Cleeve and initially produced special aviation clocks.

'The Lansdown Hotel Gang' in the 1950s. All were employed in businesses in and around Cheltenham, and were regulars at the Lansdown Hotel. Left to right: Frank Barrett (Bristol Siddeley), Mrs C. Keating (Smith's), Reg Gilroy (Bristol Siddeley), Margaret Needham (GCHQ), Ken Needham (GCHQ), Gordon Hyer (GCHQ), Frank Keating (Dowty's), Maura McCabe (GCHQ), Les Yull (GCHQ), Ernie Portman (Precision Instruments), Ian Gordon (Lansdown Hotel manager), 'Mary' (GCHQ), C. Keating (Bristol Siddeley), Sheila Keating (Rouse Co. Ltd), 'Margaret' (Lansdown Hotel barmaid).

One of the social events organized by Dowty's for their employees and their friends at the Gupshill Manor in Tewkesbury. Left to right: Bill and Flora King, Michael and Barbara Gill, Ray and Barbara Gill, Ron and Jean Harrison. Bill King and Michael Gill both worked at Dowty's, Ray Gill was a driving instructor, and Ron Harrison was the production manager at Walker Crosweller.

Another Dowty dance. At the centre table, from left to right, are: Flora King, Barbara Gill, Barbara Gill, Betty Smith, Bill King, Michael Gill, Ray Gill.

A Walker Crosweller dinner/dance at the Cheltenham Pump Rooms in the late 1950s. The couples are, left to right: Carl and Pat Bates, Ray and Barbara Gill, Ron and Jean Harrison. The musicians playing in the background are probably the Al Kessel Band, a locally famous and popular band at that time. The engineering firm Walker Crosweller moved to Cheltenham in 1937, when they built a factory in the Whaddon district. In the 1950s they employed about 500 people and produced thermostatic mixing valves.

SPORT

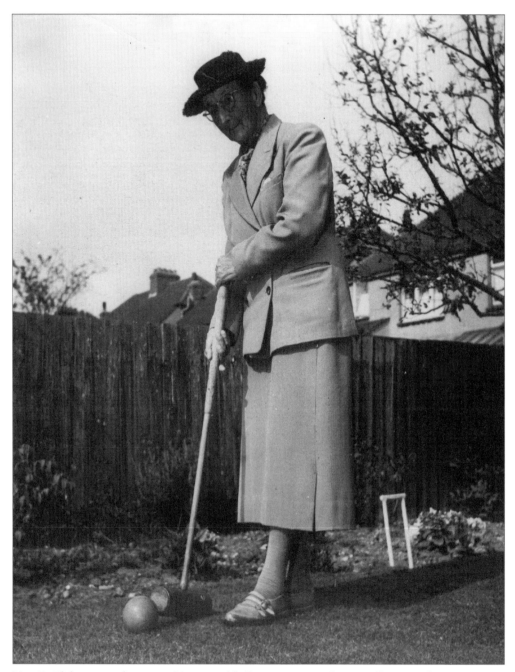

Miss E. Elphinstone playing, at 91 years old, 'better croquet than ever!', 8 October 1956. Miss Elphinstone was a long-time member of the Cheltenham Croquet Club situated in the Old Bath Road. Founded in 1869, the club shares with Brighton and the All England Club at Wimbledon the distinction of being the oldest croquet club in Britain. The 1950s saw several fluctuations in the club's fortunes. In 1953 it was virtually bankrupt but was saved by an emergency recovery programme. In 1957 electricity was supplied into the club houses and a bar was installed in 1959. The club is now of international repute with test matches being hosted regularly.

Another member of high repute was Edgar Jackson CBE, here playing on one of the club's lawns. Edgar Jackson was a noted civil servant who moved to Cheltenham in 1953 with GCHQ. He was influential in the relocation of GCHQ, and often joked that the superior facilities at Cheltenham's Croquet Club swayed his choice. He was awarded his CBE in 1953 and achieved national fame when in 1977 and 1979, aged 71 and 73, he became the oldest man to win the British Men's Championship. In the background is another club member, Lionel Ayliffe.

Cheltenham Cricket Club team, 1951. Back row, left to right: W. Peplow, E.L. Hanks, S. Walter, T.R. Smith, C.T. Hitchman, C. Gibbons. Front row: D.N. Perry, W.T. Mustoe, P.W. Woof (captain), A.G.S. Wilcox, F.J. Sewell.

Members of Cheltenham Cricket Club, 1952. Back row, left to right: H.J. Norris (umpire), T.R. Smith, S. Walter, C.H. Gibbons, D. Howarth, G. Ward, J.D. Blake, E. Preston (scorer). Front row: D.N. Perry, F.J. Sewell, P.W. Woof (captain), W.T. Mustoe, J.W. Smith. The Smith brothers, T.R. and J.W., were also renowned footballers; both played for the Cheltenham Town Football Club.

Cheltenham Cricket Club's 1953 team photographed at the newly opened St Stephen's ground clubhouse. Back row, left to right: J.C. Compton (umpire), E. Preston, F.O. Martin, W.T. Mustoe, D. Howarth, A.R. Bloodworth, D. Burge, C. Gibbons, W. Rogers (umpire), J.W. Smith. Front row: F.J. Sewell, D.N. Perry, P.W. Woof (captain), T.R. Smith. A.R. Bloodworth ran Bloodworth's seed merchants on the Bath Road, a family concern that is still thriving, selling pet supplies.

Cheltenham Cricket Club team, 1954. Back row: W. Rogers (umpire), A.R. Bloodworth, ? Ryder, W. Peplow, ? Woodward, G. Ward, D. Howarth, W. Dawson (umpire). Front row: T.R. Smith, D.N. Perry, F.J. Sewell (captain), P.W. Woof, C.H. Gibbons.

Cheltenham Town Midweek Eleven, 1955. As the name suggests, midweek teams played on Wednesday evenings and were regarded more as 'social' than their more competitive first team counterparts. Back row, left to right: A.R. Bloodworth, W.F. Dale, N. Tovey, J. Leather, H.C. Robinson, P. Brealey, H.J. Norris (umpire). Front row: F.O. Martin, A. Downes (vice-captain), E.L. Hanks (captain), J. Barnfield, C.E. Baker.

Batting for Gloucestershire in the Cheltenham College grounds in 1959 is Ronald B. Nicholls, an elegant right-handed batsman and off-break bowler who played for the county from 1951 to 1975. He made 534 appearances and scored 23,607 runs at an average of over 26. Only Hammond, Milton and Dipper have scored more runs for the county. In 1962 he scored over 2,000 runs in the season. He later played in the Western Cricket League for Cheltenham Cricket Club with his two sons Laurie and Paul, and also had two spells playing for Cheltenham Town Football Club, the first in the early 1950s and the second in 1965 and 1966.

One of Gloucestershire Cricket Club's most successful teams photographed in the Cheltenham College Grounds in the late 1950s. Back row, left to right: -?-, B. Wells, A. Brown, J. Mortimore, D. Smith, R. Nicholls, B. Meyer, F. Aubrey (scorer). Front row: C.A. Milton, T. Graveney, G. Emmett, -?-, C. Cook, M. Young. Mortimore, Smith, Graveney, Emmett and Cook all went on to play test cricket for England, Graveney gaining the most impressive record of 79 matches and scoring 4,882 runs at an average of 44.38. C.A. Milton played test cricket for England six times, and also has the distinction of having played football for his country on one occasion.

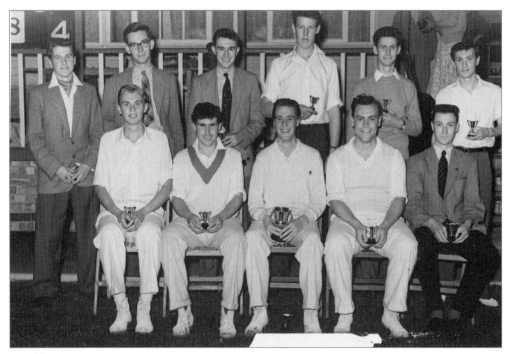

One of the Dowty's inter-departmental apprentices cricket teams in either 1956 or 1957. Back row, left to right: -?-, -?-, -?-, M. Finch, T. Smith, M. Gill. Front row: B. Eeles, G. Wakefield, D. Nourse, J. Daft, B. Scarborough.

Dowty's football team, early 1950s. Unfortunately no names have survived with this photograph.

Swindon Road Senior Boy's School football team, 1951. Back row, left to right: Mr Outhwaite (teacher), D. Turner, B. Reeves, D. Marsh, ? Collins, D. Gardner, Mr Littlewood (headmaster). Middle row: J. Gibbons, R. Mansell, B. Piff, B. Upton, T. Smith. Front row: D. Boon, B. Green, A. Liddiard. The following year Swindon Road Senior Boys' School became Elmfield School.

Cheltenham Town Football Club team of 1957/58 with the Southern League Cup. Back row, left to right: F. Carnie, J. Farrel, N. Baird, W. Gourlay, J. Geddes, J. Hyde, D. Barrett (trainer). Front row: P. Cleland, D. Fowler, R. Dunlap, R. Lewin (manager), A. Scott, C. Burder, S. Dunn.

J.M. Brown of Cheltenham College starting the 50 yards run that led to his team's second try during the match against Stowe on 22 November 1958. The college won this home fixture 11–9.

Dowty Electrics Rugby team, early 1950s.

Members of Dowty Rugby Club pose for the camera on a cold winter's morning in the early 1950s before leaving for a visit to Twickenham. Their black and white coach is on the opposite side of the road to Cheltenham's town hall and is therefore facing the wrong way for today's traffic flow.

The successful Cheltenham College cross-country team of 1959 who were unbeaten in all school matches. Back row, left to right: Mr D.J. Ellison (coach), R.T. Knights, R.D.D. Henderson, P.B. Sarase, J.C. Lewys-Lloyd. Front row: J.A. Farrington, I.B. Knights (captain), S. Drake-Wilkes, D.M. Wood.

The Smith's Industries' ladies relay team with the cups that they won during the 1949/50 season. On the left is Joan Gilroy and in the centre is the works manager, W.E. Watson.

SPECIAL EVENTS

Crowds line the streets as the royal procession bearing Princess Elizabeth arrives at Cheltenham Town Hall on Friday 15 March 1951. The Princess was welcomed at the Town Hall with a small civic reception and then her motorcade swept her up to the Cheltenham Gentlemen's College, the main destination of her visit.

The Princess with A.G. Eliot-Smith, the college's headmaster, as he escorts her to lunch. The royal visit was one of Eliot-Smith's final events at the college; he left later that year to become headmaster of Victoria College in Cairo, having been headmaster of Cheltenham College since 1940.

The Princess with prefects from the college's new block. She was initially welcomed to the school in College House, toured the buildings at the top of College Field and then went to the Hall for lunch. The college proudly states that she ate the same meal (albeit a slightly special meal) that all the boys ate in the hall.

After lunch the Princess was further escorted around the college, stopping at Thirlestaine House to inspect the model aeroplane exhibition, after which she went to see the Junior School.

Prefects B.C.J. Warren (left) and N.C. Carnegie-Brown with the Princess in the drawing room. The Princess's visit is commemorated by an inscription artistically chiselled into the stonework of the college's main building.

Queen Elizabeth, the Queen Mother, visited Cheltenham Ladies' College on 20 July 1954 as part of the celebrations to mark the centenary of the school's opening. The Queen Mother greeted and talked to pupils and staff, planted a magnolia tree in the college garden and gave a speech to the entire school in the Princess Hall.

Here the Queen Mother is being escorted around the Ladies' College by the principal, Miss J.A. Tredgold, who had taken over the post from Miss Popham the previous September. The Queen Mother so enjoyed her visit to the school that the following year she endowed an annual prize to be awarded to 'the girl who by her character and personality had contributed most to the college'.

Viscount Montgomery visited Cheltenham Gentlemen's College on 14 March 1959. On his arrival he was greeted by Mr Pentreath who was headmaster of the college from 1952 until 1959. Montgomery's visit was one of his last involvements with the school.

Escorted by CCF Sergeant-Major N.G.D. Bury, Viscount Montgomery inspects the guard of honour that welcomed him to the college on Todd's Lawn, which is situated to the west of the college chapel.

Viscount Montgomery was given a complete tour of the college including Hazelwell boarding house. In the evening he gave an address to the school in the 'Big Classical' – the main hall – in which he talked about his wartime experiences and his views on the political situation in Europe with regard to the east/west divide.

Here Montgomery casts a critical eye over the college's Combined Cadet Force, lined up for inspection. The CCF sheds in the background were situated on the corner of Sandford Road and Bath Road. This land was sold by the college in the eighties and subsequently modern, high-class apartments were built there.

The college drummers in all their splendour during Montgomery's visit in 1959.

George Dowty welcomes the French actress Leslie Caron to Arle Court, sometime in the late 1950s. Over the years Dowty's have welcomed many VIPs, including Prince Philip, The Duke of Edinburgh, to inspect its factories. Leslie Caron's visit was one of the more unusual, but perhaps more popular visits. Famed for her elfin-like figure, she starred in several major films of the 1950s and 1960s, including *Daddy Long-Legs* with Fred Astaire, and the Oscar-laden *Gigi* with Maurice Chevalier.

The Dowty truck dressed up for the Battle of Britain Week procession through the town probably in 1957. Dowty's went to great lengths to help raise funds for the Battle of Britain Appeal and it served as a reminder of both the great sacrifice of our servicemen during the war and the enormous efforts Dowty's made to produce the parts for the aircraft that finally brought us victory in the battle.

In 1957 Dowty's organized a motor rally that was held in the company's grounds. All types of vehicles were on display and prizes were given for the best in each class.

Some of the vehicles that took part in the Dowty Motor Rally of 1957.

Throughout the 1950s Dowty's maintained their flight ATC, which was open to all personnel and apprentices. Here members of the flight ATC embark on a church parade in 1958.

The prize winners of a competition, probably for best works' vehicles, on their procession around the town. It is thought to have taken place in 1958, but the location is not known because the Rotunda service station seen here has long gone. The first prize went to the Gloucestershire Dairy milk float, and second prize to a truck belonging to Barnby Bendall, the export packers and shippers, but sadly the third vehicle is indistinguishable.

The window display at the Gloucestershire Dairy Company's shop at 23 The Promenade during Carnival Week, 1957. Carnival Week ran from Saturday 7 September until Saturday 14 September, and its main purpose was to raise funds for the Battle of Britain Appeal fund. The layout of tins and the design of the display are typical of the style of window displays of the 1950s.

A garden party was held at the Ladies' College on Saturday 4 July 1953 to commemorate the centenary anniversary of the founding of the college. (The following year the college celebrated the centenary of its opening, during which the Queen Mother visited the college, *see* p. 55.) Over three thousand pupils, parents, staff and guests attended the party and it was very much the high point of a weekend dedicated to the celebration of a hundred years of educational excellence. On Friday 3 July the college held a Speech Day at which the guest speaker was Florence Horsbrugh, then Minister of Education. Finally, to round off the weekend, the college performed a centenary concert, a play entitled 'Even Such Is Time', illustrating college life through its hundred year span, and lastly a college film largely illustrating contemporary life at the Ladies' College.

The ballroom dancing medal winners from the Lister School of Dancing in 1956. The back row, third from the left, is John Woodward, and fifth from the left is Donald Jones; on the right is Gerald Boulton, with next to him Tim Reeks. Standing directly behind the table of cups and medals is Brenda Coster (née Barnes), and in the second row, third from the left, is Janet Lister.

A scene from 'To Dorothy and Son', one of the Dowty Players' productions. It was staged in 1957 at the Dowty Social Club.

During the 1950s amateur dramatics were encouraged for employees at the large Cheltenham firms. Here employees of Smith's stage their pantomime, 'Aladdin', in 1954. Left to right: -?-, -?-, Doug Williams, Bill Spragg, Les ?, -?-, Margaret ?, -?-, Jean Thomson, Brenda Barnes, -?-, -?-, -?-.

Behind the scenes of 'Aladdin' in 1954. On the left, sitting nearest the camera is Les, hunched towards the stove is Brian, to his left is Stella Thomson, then Doug Williams and Brenda Barnes.

Part of the chorus line for Smith's pantomime of 1955, 'Cinderella'. Third from the left is Jean Thomson and just behind her is Brenda Barnes.

One of Cheltenham's great characters during the 1950s was David Seccombe, alias Vladimir Lavinski, here playing the piano at a public performance. Vladimir was a well-spoken, intelligent man who unfortunately fell victim to his own eccentricities. He frequently played the piano at the town hall for balls, and believed himself to be one of the great pianists. Indeed he fancied that he was the reincarnation of Franz Liszt. As such he would parade around the town in knee-length boots, a swirling cape and a swagger stick, with a flower in each lapel. In 1952 he hit national headlines when the papers heard about his behaviour, and after this publicity he embarked on an ill-fated musical tour. The audience walked out of his performance at the Wigmore Hall in London when he added passages to Beethoven's 'Moonlight Sonata', and his career ended as abruptly as it started. He died in the early 1960s in a residential home, a very disturbed man still only in his thirties.

RESTRUCTURING THE TOWN

Reconstruction in Pittville Street, October 1954. Of particular interest is the range of shops in the High Street; between the various clothes shops of Burton's, Peter Robinson and Collins Brothers is the fishmongers MacFisheries. Today only the Burton shop remains under the same tenancy. Doris's Pittville Café, on the left, was run by Miss D. Wilks.

Looking up Pittville Street from the High Street. After the war there had been much jerry-building to provide quick, short-term accommodation for families temporarily staying in the town. The Cheltenham Society was formed at this time to ensure that the Regency heritage of the town was kept intact despite all the extra building.

'Improving' Pittville Street. One of the Cheltenham Society's more controversial decisions concerned the destruction of some of the town's less distinguished older buildings in order to concentrate resources on restoring the 'better' buildings. One side of Pittville Street was demolished (as seen here) to enable new shops to be built. Part of Saqui & Laurence Ltd, jewellers, 121 High Street, is visible on the right.

The rubble from the demolished buildings is clearly visible in this view of Pittville Street in October 1954. Notice the two Peter Robinson shops separated by Lennards. The Pittville Street 'improvements' were controlled and orchestrated by the town's borough and water engineer, G. Gould Marsland MBE.

The foundations of Sharpe and Fisher Ltd in Pittville Street were exposed during the improvements. The firm was founded in 1912 by John Fisher and Thomas Sharpe, trading from a house in Fairfield Park Road, Cheltenham. Their original Pittville Street site was acquired after a few years and remained an important outlet until it was sold in 1973. In 1955 Sharpe and Fisher had four showrooms in Pittville Street (fireplaces and sanitaryware at no. 15, domestic hardware at no. 23, china and glass at no. 27, and wallpapers and paint at nos 29 and 31). The two latter can be seen here. Sharpe and Fisher is now a national limited company with twenty-three branches.

The view from the end of Pittville Street over Albion Street and into Portland Street. Pittville Street wasn't the only town centre street to be improved in the 1950s – Winchcombe Street was similarly restructured and widened and Albion Street went through an extensive widening programme.

Pittville Street in temporary disarray, October 1954. Soon a new foundation would be laid for the street, and modern shop buildings would replace the older buildings that were unfortunately deemed too expensive to renovate. To the left of Burton's on the High Street is J. Sears' shoe shop – home of the True-form Boot Company.

This double-decker bus at the Royal Well bus station is about to set off on its trip to Staverton and the Hare and Hounds at Churchdown. Note the white steering wheel – this was to remind the drivers that they were now driving new, wider vehicles: instead of the 7ft 6in buses they were used to, the new vehicles were 8ft 2½ in wide. Soon the Royal Well bus station itself would undergo a restructuring programme.

Shortly before the renovation of the Royal Well bus terminus, LAE 28 stands outside the Regal Cinema (now replaced by Royscot House), facing the wrong way for today's traffic flow.

In 1954, as the town sought to modernize itself, the Royal Well bus terminus became the centre of attention. These next few photographs were all taken in March 1954 and illustrate how the terminus looked before work commenced on creating the sheltered waiting areas for bus passengers.

Cars were much in evidence, parked around the Royal Crescent (in the background) and all around the small park that separates the Crescent from the rest of Royal Well. Just visible on the far right is the taxi hut.

The bus shelters at the 'bottom' of the park area can just be seen on the left of this picture, by the telephone box. Here buses would collect and deposit their fares.

Looking up Royal Well Road from behind the Regal Cinema, March 1954. The road was named after the spa well which was discovered in about 1716 to have medicinal properties and which was visited and used by the ailing King George III in 1788. The original well now rests underneath the Princess Hall of the Cheltenham Ladies' College.

The view from Royal Crescent through the trees to Royal Well Road. Behind the taxi rank (left) is the old *Gloucestershire Echo* office. Also visible is the YMCA hut, built during the Second World War specifically to provide a canteen for both servicemen and members of the public, utilizing local produce.

Looking down on the Royal Well bus terminus from the back of the Municipal Offices, this picture gives a good indication of the layout of the terminus before its renovation. The buses only used the south end of the road at the bottom of the park area. The plan was to build a line of bus shelters extending up the road and around towards Royal Well Crescent.

This photograph was taken from the same place as the one above, but the photographer has turned slightly to show the corner of Royal Well Road with its taxi rank, Marguerite's (florist and fruiter) on the corner of Crescent Terrace and Clarence Parade, and a part of Clarence Parade (right).

By June 1954 work was under way on building the new Royal Well bus terminus. The pictures on these two pages were taken between 16 and 18 June and show the first stages of a development that would take almost a year to complete.

Much of the park area was levelled and cleared, and many of the young trees were chopped down. Here a small bulldozer levels the 'inside' of what will be the new terminus.

Despite the rain the workers pressed on with the foundation plans; already the shape of the new terminus is becoming evident.

Another view of the building site.

By May 1955 the terminus was almost completed and was already in use. The park area has been reduced to a few trees and some grass.

Looking modern, new and clean the Royal Well bus terminus was a great improvement on its predecessor. Cheltenham now had a focal point for bus and coach travellers both entering and leaving the town. At this time the buses were only using the 'inside' of the shelters to pick up and drop off fares, while cars were still parked around the outside.

This view shows that traffic continued to flow both ways at this time, although today traffic only travels northwards down this road (i.e. from top to bottom in this picture). Despite so much preparation, planning and expenditure, only forty years later the bus shelters are now very dated, and in a poor state of repair. Despite efforts to restore some of their former glory, it seems their days are now numbered.

The top of the YMCA hut is visible on the left of this picture behind the flat roof. The chapel seen at top right, with a bus parked outside, is now the home of Hobbs and Chambers, auctioneers.

Buses waiting at the newly completed Royal Well bus terminus, May 1955.

A new Bristol Lodekka waiting at Royal Well, 1955. This bus was so new that its destination linens hadn't yet been fitted. Behind it is a Bristol K type bus, probably loading for Tewkesbury. This is an older vehicle, probably dating from just before the war. Both these buses were part of the Bristol Tramways fleet.

Taken on Monday 29 July 1957, the final pictures in this section illustrate the demolition of the traffic island and public conveniences in St George's Square, down the Lower High Street. In the background is the furniture repository of Dicks & Sons. It was originally a chapel built for Protestant dissenters in the early nineteenth century; at one time the founder of the penny post, Sir Rowland Hill, came to preach there.

The view down the Lower High Street with the demolition work in progress. The public conveniences were later rebuilt on the pavement adjacent to the bowling green where they still stand today.

Two final views of the work to demolish the traffic island and public conveniences. It was hoped that this would ease the flow of traffic down the High Street, and that, with the relocation of the public conveniences to the pavement, there would be less unnecessary crossing of the road by pedestrians.

THE BUILDING OF HESTER'S WAY

No. 93 Hawthorn Road, the newly constructed home of Vic and Audrey Kent, pictured in 1952. The early 1950s saw an extensive building programme in Cheltenham as the town attempted to house its rapidly increasing population. The development was mainly focused on Hester's Way, between Tewkesbury Road and Gloucester Road. Hawthorn Road was one part of the new development.

The ground behind Hawthorn Road was still uncultivated. In the background can just be seen Princess Elizabeth Way, which runs the length of Hester's Way, cutting it almost in half. The building programme engulfed this major road on both sides with approximately three thousand homes, varying from huge blocks of flats to semi-detached, two-storey houses. A shopping precinct, Coronation Square, was built at the same time to give Hester's Way the feel of a town within a town.

These photographs show work in progress on the Hester's Way estate around Princess Elizabeth Way, in February/March 1953. As well as the new shopping centre, schools were provided for the increased population, and Cheltenham's second Roman Catholic church, St Thomas More's, a modern hexagonal building, was also added. The council housing programme had originally started before the war, but had to be delayed because of hostilities. When the war ended the council finished its programme at Lynworth, near Whaddon, and then turned its attention to Hester's Way and Princess Elizabeth Way in 1952.

The buildings taking shape. By the time the council had finished these developments in the 1960s they owned over seven thousand houses and flats, five and a half thousand of which had been built after the war. The housing shortage was largely brought about as a result of the incredible success of Cheltenham's engineering businesses, in particular Dowty's and Smith's. Workers had temporarily moved to the town during the war to take up positions with the companies, but after the war many wanted to stay and therefore needed more permanent residences. The firms' continuing expansion also brought more people into the town.

The blocks of flats grew and grew. Various building methods were used in Hester's Way. The traditional bricks and mortar technique shown here was complemented by the more modern method shown overleaf. The trees in the background are a reminder of the planes, chestnuts and oaks that were probably planted during the Regency period and which had to be removed to allow the town to expand.

The creation of the skyline of modern Cheltenham in Hester's Way. In the rush to erect the new estates, little thought was given to the destruction of the town's open spaces. Whole farms around Benhall and Arle were swallowed up in the development which, like the Royal Well bus terminus, is already looking dated and is threatened with destruction and renewal.

These four photographs illustrate the revolutionary method of construction used in building the high-rise blocks of flats along Princess Elizabeth Way. The method was known as 'no fines', which essentially referred to the fact that the cement used in the building was not mixed with sand but with gravel.

The first stage involved the building of a shuttered framework, one storey at a time, into which the cement and gravel mixture was poured. The success of the method lay in its speed and cost efficiency: the foundations and three storeys could be built in a matter of days. It was much quicker and cheaper than employing builders using bricks and mortar.

Here the cement and gravel mixture is poured into the building framework of one of the high-rise blocks on the east side of the northern part of Princess Elizabeth Way in 1953. Once the mixture had set, the building really only needed a few finishing touches.

The completed framework of a two-storey building in Hester's Way, built by the 'no fines' method. Bricks were used for interior walls and chimney-stacks, but everything else was cement and gravel, creating a very coarse exterior.

Still surrounded by fields, Hester's Way began to take shape in early 1953. Soon the estates of Rowanfield, St Mark's, Arle and Hester's Way would become indistinguishable; Benhall was 'saved' only by the intervention of the Gloucester Road.

Such was the urgency of the situation that almost as soon as the buildings were completed families moved in. The need for local schools was equally pressing, hence the construction of Hester's Way Junior and Infants Schools, Monkscroft School and the eventual relocation of the Boys' Grammar School to the area.

The houses and flats of Barbridge Road almost ready for habitation in 1953. Despite the growth of urban Cheltenham, some precious open spaces were retained and remain today. They include the Hester's Way park at the south end of Princess Elizabeth Way, a playing field off Welch Road and some smaller public open spaces, a reminder of the open farmland that once existed there.

Lechmere Road, viewed from Princess Elizabeth Way. Even with building work still very much in evidence, the children and curtains indicate that these houses are already occupied.

The finishing touches to the brick-built blocks of flats on Princess Elizabeth Way. This is probably Edward Wilson House or Scott House, while on the opposite side of the road can be found Quebec, Canada and Montreal Houses, all very similar blocks of flats.

As well as Dowty's and Smith's, people moved into Cheltenham to work for other companies, notably Eagle Star and Royal Insurance, the universities admission council and, on a larger scale, GCHQ. All of these had relocated to the town in the 1950s. GCHQ moved to Cheltenham in 1952, taking over two sites at Oakley and Benhall that had been used in the war and were at the time full of Nissen huts. This photograph shows the construction of GCHQ buildings at one of those sites, probably Oakley.

The Benhall GCHQ site in 1953, surrounded by wire fencing. Both Oakley and Benhall were built to similar specifications, mainly one-storey buildings very much in the style of the Nissen huts that they replaced. Benhall Farm had been taken over during the war by the Americans for the Forces of Supply, and it was they who constructed the first huts on the site. After the war it seemed a natural progression for GCHQ to take over the site, once it had been decided that they would relocate to Cheltenham from Bletchley Park.

The entrance to GCHQ at Oakley. The Oakley and Benhall sites would have been similar in appearance, and although they are on opposite sides of the town the two sites are really a single entity. To house the civil servants and their families who moved with GCHQ to Cheltenham, the council provided five hundred new homes and about the same number of single flats.

Oakley GCHQ. Note the 'temporary' prefabricated houses on the left, which were very much a short-term solution to the housing problem after the war. The council worked hard to replace them.

AROUND THE TOWN

The view up Lower High Street towards the High Street, late 1950s. The Boys' Grammar School is in the middle of the left hand side.

The tower of the Boys' Grammar School was reminiscent of the gate tower of Corpus Christi College, Oxford. This building was constructed between 1887 and 1889 to plans by local architects Knight & Chatters. The site belonged to the Fellows of Corpus Christi College, under Pate's Foundation of 1586, until they sold it in the mid-1960s. It was demolished in 1967.

The magnificent entrance to the grammar school. The site is now home to Sainsbury's, the classical architecture of the nineteenth century exchanged for the modernistic and characterless architecture of the 1960s.

Proudly watching over the students entering his schoolhouse is Richard Pate, the founder of the Boys' Grammar School in Cheltenham. His statue remains in the present grammar school in Princess Elizabeth Way and is the only part of the High Street building to have survived. Today's grammar school is a mixed sex school, the boys' and girls' grammar schools having amalgamated in 1986. The boys' school moved in the mid-1960s into another building which survived less than thirty years and is now awaiting demolition. A new building was erected on the same site and opened in 1995.

Tinkler's, the old basket shop at 168 High Street, *c.* 1950. The shop specialized in wicker baskets and bags and was first established in the town in 1816. It closed in the late 1950s or early 1960s and the shop was demolished in 1963.

Bound for the cemetery at Prestbury, FAD 251 waits outside Martin's dry cleaners in the High Street. Behind it a small group of grammar school boys sit on the steps of their school after a hard day's work.

This double-decker bus is just leaving the one-way section of the High Street on its way to the new housing estate at Lynworth. On the left is Dickins', tobacconists.

The view down Pittville Street from Portland Street, before the demolition and 'improvements' had taken place in the early 1950s.

The view up Pittville Street from the High Street end: compare this with the picture at the top of page 67. Note the two policemen on point duty. There was a daily police patrol around the High Street and Pittville Street, and since shortly before the war a policeman had patrolled the Promenade to ensure that 'inappropriate' elements of society and unacceptable behaviour were kept out. This patrol, which often involved two policemen, was established after complaints were made about young couples openly courting in shop doorways on Sunday afternoons!

Another view of Pittville Street before its partial destruction, probably in October 1954.

All the properties on the left of Pittville Street were swept away by 1955. Sidney C. Rawlings' bookshop at no. 17, just visible on the right, was sandwiched between Sharpe and Fisher and the Sydney Arms Hotel, the proprietor of which was Cyril Richards.

The junction of the High Street and Pittville Street. Where MacFisheries, Collins Brothers, Peter Robinson and Lennards used to stand, we now have the Intersport shop and Virgin Megastore. The Cake Basket's van is parked outside their shop, at 1 and 3 Pittville Street.

Winchcombe Street, which runs across the centre of this picture, September 1957. Shortly after this picture was taken nos 23 and 24 Winchcombe Street (Jackson's pork purveyors and M.E. Barnes, newsagent) were demolished to make way for the widening of Albion Street. The man crossing Albion Street shows how narrow it was. Traffic could not enter from this end, the flow of traffic being the opposite to what it is today.

Winchcombe Street, looking towards the Gaumont Palace Cinema, in 1957. The cinema first opened on 6 March 1933 and was built on the site of the former Highbury Chapel. It became the Odeon on 16 December 1962, the name it has kept ever since as Cheltenham's only surviving cinema. In the 1950s the town had several cinemas, including the Regal by the Royal Well bus station, the Colosseum in Albion Street and the Daffodil in Suffolk Parade. W.J. Oldacre's, millers, corn and seed merchants, was at 31 Winchcombe Street. Their painted gable sign is still partly visible today, but Oldacre's building is now the Axiom Centre.

The view down Winchcombe Street from opposite the Gaumont towards Albion Street. In the 1950s all the street signs were spelt Winchcomb, but in recent years the modern spelling has been adopted, although a few signs dating from this period have survived.

A.A. Motors in North Place, probably in the very late 1950s. Most of these buildings have now been demolished to make way for the ever-widening road systems. The building with the columns and steps, and the lamppost outside (formerly the Countess of Huntingdon's Connexion chapel), is one of the few remaining premises, which today is used as a gymnasium.

A double-decker bus on its way from the High Street to the Promenade, late 1950s. The new buildings at the end of Pittville Street are clearly visible in the centre. Note the policeman on Promenade point duty. In earlier times, the top of the Promenade (from the Midland Bank) was known as 'The Colonnade'. Today this point is generally referred to as 'Boots' Corner'.

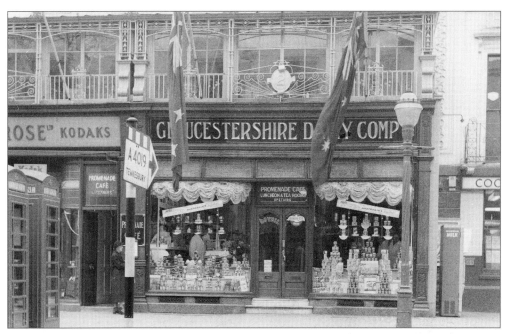

The Gloucestershire Dairy Company's shop with above it the cafeteria, in the Promenade, 1950s. On the left is the recently closed Will R. Rose, photographer, and on the right the old corner site of Thomas Cook's before it moved to the High Street in the 1980s.

A view down the Promenade. The lady on the right is buying a carton of flavoured milk from the dispensing machine. An innovation of the 1950s, the dispensers proved very popular and several were to be found around the town.

This Benhall-bound bus travelling down the Colonnade into the Promenade. It is about to pass the premises of A. Whitcombe, fine art dealers, just visible on the right.

A sunny Sunday afternoon in Montpellier Gardens in the late 1950s. The bandstand is being used by a local band, entertaining the people relaxing in the municipal deckchairs.

Queen's Circus, photographed from just outside the Queen's Hotel (now known just as 'The Queen's'). Note the sign, long since lost, to St Andrew's Presbyterian Church on the corner. None of the businesses shown here (which include Morgan's, grocers, and Hayman's, jewellers and silversmiths) has survived, except for F.C. Dodwell & Sons, stationers, who are still very much in business, but are now in premises on the Bath Road. The Dodwell family has a long history of business in the town, including an interest in Martin's jewellers in the Promenade.

Park House in Thirlestaine Road, the home from 1954 of Edgar Jackson (see p. 41). He bought the house from Mr and Mrs Grundy and later, using his skills and training as an architect, he divided the house into two, the Old Bath Lodge being the other residence.

'Old Classical', the main hall of the Cheltenham Gentlemen's College with its new stage and decor in 1950. The assembly hall was designed by the college's own resident architect, Louis de Soissons, who had been at the college since 1938. Among his other notable achievements was the design of the college's library in the 'Big Modern' part of the building. This library was a gift to the college by Major J.S. Iredell in memory of his grandfather, Captain J.S. Iredell, a co-founder of the college. Louis de Soissons died in the summer of 1962 having achieved fame for his talents not just in Cheltenham but nationally and internationally as well.

The junction of the Evesham Road and Church Road (from the right) at the war memorial in Bishops Cleeve. The war memorial has since been moved to the opposite end of the village and the lovely old thatched cottages on the corner of Church Road have been demolished to make way for the modern, utilitarian buildings that presently house a chip shop, a Chinese take-away, a video shop and an off-licence. The thatched building on the right, the King's Head public house, has thankfully survived.

Joe Powers' dilapidated petrol station on the Evesham Road in Bishops Cleeve. It was situated just about where the opening to Gilder's Paddock is now. Joe Powers himself is standing by the pumps. Long after the garage closed these sheds remained, gradually collapsing until they were finally cleared some time in the 1980s. Opposite the garage was Gilder's butcher shop, which was located between what is now Home Farm and Budgens' car park.

The proprietors of Edginton & Son's bakehouse pose for the camera outside their premises in Tobyfield Road, Bishops Cleeve. The site is now occupied by the Somerfield and Co-op supermarkets.

The view along School Road from its junction with Church Road, Bishops Cleeve, in the early 1950s. Just off to the left is the square into which the war memorial was moved in order to ease traffic flow along the Evesham Road.

In the late 1950s the expansion of Bishops Cleeve began to have an impact, with old buildings being pulled down to make way for modern homes and modern shops. The Swallow pub (far left) was built at this time, as were the bank and the line of shops with flats above running down the right side of this picture.

'The Green' in Bishops Cleeve. P. Smith newsagents, the fourth shop from the right, remains in business today. The Green has since lost its grass and is now reduced to a tarmacked car park.

The success and expansion of Smith's Industries in Bishops Cleeve during and after the war caused a serious housing shortage. The company collaborated with the Cheltenham Rural District Council to create the Bishops Cleeve Housing Association. During the war the initial development was in Meadoway, but in the 1950s the housing estate programme developed throughout the village. These are the new homes in Bishops Drive.

Tobyfield Road, another new road built by the Bishops Cleeve House Association. The aim of the project was to construct houses as a continuation of the village but without spoiling its old world charm. Note the absence of traffic problems!

CHELTENHAM FROM ABOVE

Cheltenham in the late 1950s. The main road running into the town from the bottom left is Lansdown
Road, with Lansdown Crescent arcing around behind it. On the left, about halfway up the picture, is the
impressive Christ Church, with behind it the old St James's railway station. On the right halfway up the

picture we can see Montpellier Gardens, and, beyond, Montpellier Road and the tree-lined Promenade running south to north adjacent to the gardens.

West Cheltenham from the air. Dean Close School is the impressive cluster of buildings towards the top, with its playing fields below it. The Lansdown Road runs vertically down the right side of the picture,

crossing the railway bridge and leading on to the old Lansdown Castle. Hatherley Road is the main road running down the left of the picture. Little now remains of the open spaces and proliferation of fields.

Cheltenham from Leckhampton Hill, 1958. In the foreground is the 'Devil's Chimney', a limestone stack once believed to have formed naturally as the surrounding stone eroded. However, it is generally agreed today that the stack is man-made, probably by the men who worked in the quarries on the hill during the early nineteenth century. The houses visible on the right at the top of the picture are on the western side of Leckhampton.

Another view of Cheltenham from Leckhampton Hill, 30 August 1958. The straight Leckhampton Road stretches away from the middle of the picture in a north-westerly direction. Charlton Kings is on the right.

Another view from Leckhampton Hill, with Charlton Kings in the background.

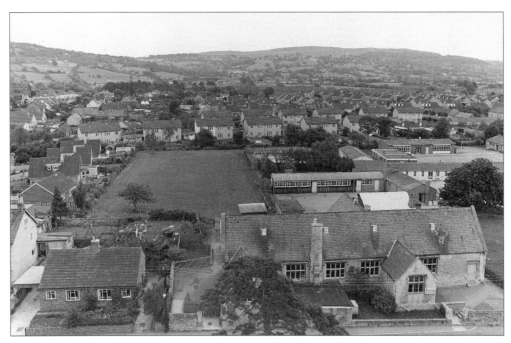

Bishops Cleeve photographed from the church tower in the 1950s. In the immediate foreground is the old school, long before the new primary and comprehensive schools were built.

Again photographed from the church tower, this is the other side of Bishops Cleeve, looking north-west. Note the numbers of thatched and older-style cottages, many of which have disappeared or have been swallowed up in the modern estates. The main road is Station Road.

An aerial photograph of Bishops Cleeve at a time when the housing developments were well under way. The road running from right to left in the foreground is the Evesham Road, with Two Hedges Road leading off it on the right just above the trees. The tithe barn is visible on the left, with the church a little way behind it.

Bishops Cleeve, probably in the late fifties. The church is clearly visible just right of centre. The fields of Homelands Farm between Bishops Cleeve and Gotherington stretch across the background.

This picture shows almost the whole of Bishops Cleeve in the very late 1950s. Two Hedges Road comes in halfway up the left side of the picture and leads across the middle of the picture, passing just behind the school and then over the railway line. Kayte Lane comes in from the bottom left and joins Two Hedges

Road. Delabere Road leads off Kayte Lane along the bottom of the picture, with Ellenborough Road running parallel behind it. The church can be seen towards the top, left of centre.

Gotherington in the late 1950s, when it was a very small and largely undeveloped village. New houses on 'The Lawns' can be seen on the right. The village shop and post office haven't yet been built, but Moat

Farm in Malleson Road is visible on the left. The War Memorial can be seen at the village's main T-junction and just beyond it, on the right, is the old school. Gretton Road runs away into the distance.

ACKNOWLEDGEMENTS

It is with sincere appreciation that I offer my thanks to the following people, without whose contributions, advice and knowledge this book would not have been possible:

Mr F. Barnes • Mrs J. Burrows • Mr Sewell and Cheltenham Cricket Club • Mrs E. Magee and Cheltenham Croquet Club • Mr Cook and Cheltenham Football Club • Mr T. Pearce and Cheltenham Gentlemen's College • Mrs J. Johnstone and Cheltenham Ladies' College • Mrs B. Coster • Mr H.C. Denham • Dowty Aerospace • Mr B. Elliott • Mr & Mrs R.A. Gill • Mrs J. Gilroy • The *Gloucestershire Echo* Mrs J. Harrison • Mrs Jackson, Mr J. Keithleigh and Cheltine Ltd • Mr & Mrs V. Kent • Mr R. King The C.F. Martin Collection • Mrs P. Nicholls • Mr H. Osmond and Dean Close School • Mr W. Potter Mrs B. Smith • Mr B. Stephens and Smith's Industries • Mr D. Toms.

And especially to my wife Jayne, who is and will always be my best friend.

To any people I have omitted to mention I offer my apologies and my thanks. Please note that every effort has been made to contact and establish copyright holders of all photographs.

The Dowty Resident Dance Band at the Dowty Social Club in the 1950s.

BRITAIN IN OLD PHOTOGRAPHS

To order any of these titles please telephone our distributor, Littlehampton Book Services on 01903 721596
For a catalogue of these and our other titles please ring Regina Schinner on 01453 731114